I [enjoy]ed this little
bo[ok so] much (rather one
les[son] and wanted to
share some beautiful
thoughts with you.
A very special thank
you to you and Carl
for all you did to
make Cathy and Rick's
wedding so perfect.
The reception was
beautiful!
    I love you,
        Laurie
June 1979

This Morning I Held a Rose

This Morning I Held a Rose

Warmhearted Writings
About the Little Things
That Bring Us Happiness

Written by Tina Hacker

Illustrated by Anne Jaeschke

HALLMARK EDITIONS

The Little Things: AN INTRODUCTION

A neighbor asked me recently if I was happy. "Sure I'm happy," I answered quickly. "My car just passed its fifty-thousand-mile checkup."

"No, be serious," she said. "What makes you happy, really happy?"

I thought for a few moments and then suggested, "I made a good cup of coffee this morning. What could be more satisfying than that — especially at 8:00 a.m.?"

"Oh, you're hopeless," she chided as we both laughed.

But later, I began to wonder: What does make me happy? Of course, big things count, like having someone to love, good friends, a job that challenges me, a place I like to come home to. But these often get lost in the day-to-day routine of life. My happiness is made up mostly of the little things I enjoy, such as watching a sparrow, building a snowman, sleeping late on Saturday, chatting with a friend, even eating a hot dog at the ball game. Precious moments like these make me feel good inside and help me get through the day. Taken separately, none of them make much of a difference in my life. But without them, there would be all the difference in the world.

Our lives are filled with these little moments of fun and happiness. Sometimes we have to look for them, sometimes we have to create them, sometimes others bring them to us, but they're always close by. They're as near as the sunrise we see outside our window, the garden that blooms under our care, or the smile of a child who lives next door.

This Morning I Held a Rose

Some people have a knack for growing plants. Under their expert care, ferns and geraniums, African violets and begonias flourish. Ivy dances gracefully around the sides of their windows, and terrariums burst into jungles. Despite my best efforts, this talent for nurturing greenery has eluded me. I try. I really try, but most of my plants don't last very long. I had been contemplating giving up altogether and buying myself a nice green plastic garden when a friend gave me a miniature rose bush to plant. I protested, but she insisted I accept it. "You can grow it," she said and handed me some instructions. "Just follow these."

I took the plant. I watered it, fed it vitamins, protected it from the cold and whispered sweet nothings in its direction when no one was listening. Finally, after waiting and worrying and thinking, "Nothing is going to happen, nothing at all," the plant began to bud. A few weeks later it gave me a rose.

It would have been so easy to give up. Now, whenever I find myself stopping short of some goal, I remember that rose and it gives me confidence. A rose is a very handy thing to hold in your heart.

Visiting The Mailbox

A trip to the mailbox fills me with a pleasant prickle of anticipation. What will be there? Maybe I've won a raffle or the bank has discovered a large error in my favor! Even if these dreams don't come true (and they haven't so far), there always seems to be something intriguing in the mailbox: a newspaper telling us what's happening in the neighborhood, a brochure from the community college, or a letter from our congressman informing us how he's voted. Even junk mail can be interesting if it's colorful enough. Booklets describing the wonders of a boat we can build in our own living room or pamphlets filled with ads for encyclopedias may not tempt me much. But they're often amusing, informative and thought-provoking.

Of course, the very best mail is the letters and notes we get from relatives and friends, postcards from people on vacation and cards when we're celebrating a birthday or a holiday.

You might argue that I'm forgetting the bills. They aren't much fun, it's true. But we do know they are coming, so there's usually no unpleasant surprise. And many bills these days carry along ads or cheery little newsletters that at least try to soften the blow.

All things considered, the mailbox is a little daily treasure-house within our reach. And what a cheery place to visit!

Miracles Still Happen

The morning started like any other. Got up, brushed my teeth, washed my face and then pondered "The Question." Should I get on the scale and weigh myself or shouldn't I? Slowly my toe sidled up to the edge of it. Then quickly I drew it away. "What an ugly contraption," I thought. "So old fashioned. It probably isn't even accurate. I don't want to bother with it today anyway."

Still, I paused, knowing I was fighting a never-ending losing battle. Preparing myself for the worst, I valiantly stepped on the scale.

"Three pounds," I gasped. "I've lost three pounds and I wasn't even on a diet this week."

What a lovely way to begin the day. What a charming little scale. It looks so nice there, you know. All white and gleamy. It's so quaint.

The radio may blare out disasters and misfortune, but I doubt if anything could dampen the spirits of the "on-again-off-again" dieters of the world who have just discovered, by some miracle, that they have lost three pounds.

A Penny From Heaven

Something made me stop and look closer. There...on the curb. It was small and shiny. At first, I thought it was a piece of glass. But no, it was perfectly round. I leaned over and picked it up. "It's a penny!"

I know a penny will hardly buy a stick of gum these days. But there's something very special about finding one anyway — something that makes me feel I've won the sweepstakes. It's like getting a present even though it isn't your birthday. Or maybe the fun comes from knowing that out of all the people who walked right over that very penny, you spotted it first. As if fate had entered your life, you were destined to have it.

A friend of mine marks the pennies she discovers with paint or nail polish and won't ever spend them. She insists they bring her good luck. I'm not convinced of that, but I must admit when I do find a penny, I'm dimly aware of it lying in my purse all through the day. I usually save the pennies I find for at least a week. Who knows? Perhaps thinking we're going to be lucky makes it so!

In Balance

My math teacher was right. She told me I'd be sorry if I didn't learn the multiplication tables or commit the rules for decimals to memory. I think of her sage advice at least once a month — on the day my bank statement arrives. This particular day is my own moment of truth. No matter how hard I try to pretend it's not so, the day of reckoning is upon me. There is no escape. I must balance my checkbook.

Out come the pen and paper, the eraser, and sometimes a candy bar or two just to make the whole messy job a bit more bearable. Then calculations begin.

"Let's see now," I think. "Mark off the checks that have been cancelled, note the ones that haven't been recorded on the statement. Subtract — no add — come on, be brave! Compare your figures with the bank's."

I pause. "Just a minute. Something is wrong. No. Nothing is wrong. Nothing at all! Wow! It balances — right to the last penny!"

This must be how an athlete feels after winning a gold medal! Well...not exactly. But for those of us who count on our fingers and toes, a balanced checkbook is a real victory.

Monday It Isn't

Getting up early in the morning is one of the tribulations of civilization. One morning last week, as I rolled over and glanced out the window, I realized the inevitable was about to happen. The alarm clock would be ringing out the news in its own screechy way that it was time — ugh — to get up.

"Well, maybe I've got a few more minutes left," I thought as I buried my head in the pillow, refusing to look that clock in the face. "Maybe it won't go off at all. Maybe a fuse blew or — hey — just a minute. It's Saturday!"

Relief came floating over me like the warmth from a fire on a frosty day. *Saturday.* Can there be a more beautiful word, especially at seven o'clock in the morning?

The Gift Of Friendship

It began last September. Every morning as I left for work, a little boy passed my house on his way to school. At first I merely nodded a greeting and he stared shyly back. But soon we began to exchange hellos and smiles. A warm friendship grew as we got into the nice habit of stopping for a few minutes each day just to chat. I learned all about his school and he learned about my job. If I stayed home for a day, on the following morning he'd ask if I was feeling all right. And when I left early and missed our meeting, the day wouldn't seem quite complete. Like a birthday without a cake, there was something missing.

Our early-morning conversations continued all year until June, when school let out for the summer. I remember our last one. "Hello, Bill," I said as he walked by. "I bet you're getting ready for summer vacation now."

"I'm going to camp," he replied brightly. "Are you going anywhere?"

"No," I answered, thinking that an adult's lot must seem grim indeed. "I have to work. But I hope you have fun at camp. See you in the fall."

"Thanks," he said and ran off.

The following morning, as I prepared to leave the house, I noticed a package lying on the stoop. It was a bottle of cologne all wrapped up in tissue with a note that read, "From Billy — Sorry you can't go to camp."

As I took in the fragrance of the cologne, I had to hold back tears. What a precious gift friendship is.

Bells Are Not Ringing

Alexander Graham Bell — we thank you. At least most of the time. The telephone is a wonderful invention. Without it, I wouldn't be able to talk to my mother in Chicago or my aunt in Detroit. I couldn't keep in touch with my friends half so well, travel so conveniently or shop so quickly. I make and break reservations, appointments, business agreements, all by telephone.

But sometimes it seems as if the telephone is actually *ruling* my life. Who can resist answering it? Last month, I tried...and lost. The phone rang once. "I'm not going to pick it up tonight," I resolved. It rang twice. "Hmmmm, who could it be?" Three times. "Maybe it's an emergency." Ring number four. "Someone's spotted a burglar outside and is trying to warn me!" On the fifth ring, the phone won. "No," I answered the party on the other end. "I don't have a dog." Click!

A few days later, I tried to resist the lure of the phone once again. This time I won. It rang at three different times, a few minutes apart, but I refused to get disturbed, or at least, disturbed very much. I figured that anyone who wanted to reach me badly enough would try again the next day. And as for the bad news — that could always wait.

This mechanized world we live in is marvelous, and I'd be the last person to knock it. But we have to reaffirm our control over the machines — at least once in a while!

At Sunrise

The sky looked like a stained-glass window. Every inch of it seemed to be painted with a different color, and yet the colors blended together as if they were part of a planned design.

Of course, not all sunrises are brilliantly beautiful. Often enough, however, the dawn will give us a present. When this happens, I feel very close to God. I find a special reassurance watching that echo of the first Creation, and its loveliness fills my morning with joy.

The Shoe Repair Man

Like most of my neighbors, I do much of my shopping at centers that seem to be getting larger and larger every year. They're handy, and I like the excitement of all the different shops and faces and the thousands of products for sale. But I miss that personal touch when markets weren't quite so "super" and a shopping center meant five stores at the end of the block.

Luckily for me, I live in a neighborhood where some small independent stores still flourish. There's a dress shop, a yarn goods store, a bakery and Mr. Barton's shoe repair shop. Mr. Barton is the kind of "shoemaker" we read about in storybooks. He's a cozy sort of man — short and rather plump with a smile like Santa Claus. To the casual observer, his shop is a shambles, with shoes lying everywhere, not to mention laces, odd heels and jars of glue and polish. But this chaos doesn't seem to bother Mr. Barton at all. He knows exactly where everything is and claims never to have misplaced a shoe in over thirty years of business.

I've taken several pairs to him and he always has a kind word to say to me. "Are you enjoying the weather?" or "The bakery is having a special on doughnuts, don't miss it." Mr. Barton really cares

18

about people. He won't even attempt to fix a shoe he feels is beyond help. "I could try and fix it," I heard him say to a customer, "but it probably won't last too long. Don't waste your money."

Just last week, I went into his shop to pick up a shoe whose sole had needed regluing. "How much will that be?" I asked.

"Well, how much do you think it should be?" he questioned me back.

Puzzled, I suggested seventy-five cents.

"Nope," he replied firmly. "Not right."

"Uh, how about a dollar???"

"How about fifty cents?" he countered with a grin.

The Mr. Bartons of the world teach us what caring is all about.

Snowperson

Every winter needs a snowman, or should I say
snowperson? "Why does a figure made out of snow
always have to be male?" I thought last winter after a
particularly good snowfall. So I called up some friends,
and we met in my front yard to build our unique
female creation.

We managed to mold a girlish shape pretty quickly.
The real challenge came in creating our snowlady's
face. No coal eyes for our girl. Anne had brought two
lovely emerald buttons for just that purpose. (Don't
all heroines have flashing green eyes?) Next came the
nose. The pink, cone-shaped, perfume bottle we used
would have done Cleopatra proud. We added a large,
red, plastic pair of lips and then covered our lady's
head with a stringy yellow mop. She needed just one
more thing — eyelashes — and Joyce had the honor of
veiling her eyes with a pair that was over an inch long.
Our snowwoman, named "Libby," was beautiful.

As we stood and admired our handiwork, we felt as
if we were children again. More important, like
children, we saw through an old stereotype. Yes, every
winter needs a snowman — and a snowwoman, too!

Baby Love

Cousin Kristin, age six months, does not cry very often. But when she does, she's a real pro at it. Last week was her time to give her vocal chords a workout. No one could figure out why. She wasn't hungry. There were no pins sticking her. She had taken her nap and was dry. Still — Kristin was bawling her head off.

Her mother rocked her and cooed soft sounds in her ears. Still she cried. Aunt Blanche tried to appease her with a favorite rattle. No help at all. My cousin Donna attempted to play patty-cake. Donna was dismissed with a disgusted squeal and a frown. No one was in Kristin's favor that day.

"Why don't *you* hold her for a while," my aunt suggested.

"Me?" I muttered as the baby was placed in my reluctant arms. "But I'm not very good with babies, I —" And then, there was a loud silence. Kristin had stopped crying and was playfully grabbing for the buttons on my sweater. "Awwww, isn't she cute," I said, the crying spell instantly forgotten. Throughout the afternoon, I was the only relative Kristin would have anything to do with. She'd give a warning sniffle every time someone else came near.

Finally, when she drifted off to sleep, her mother tucked her into her crib for a nap. "Sorry," my aunt apologized, "Kristin kept you busy all afternoon."

"But I didn't mind at all," I answered. And I realized I wasn't saying that just to be polite. I loved every minute I held that baby. After all, I was singled out from the whole crowd. What an honor! If Kristin were the President shaking my hand, I couldn't have been more pleased.

There are many kinds of flattery in the world. And sometimes the biggest flatterers of them all weigh only eighteen pounds!

Watching Sparrows

People are always talking about the brilliant beauty of cardinals and bluejays. These bright-colored birds are like exotic ornaments that make us catch our breath at their loveliness. But I like watching sparrows best. When I see them on my lawn, I feel all is right with the world. I am at peace.

It's true that sparrows are pretty plain looking. But like many of the everyday things that surround us, they are dear for their familiar and reassuring presence. Sparrows are like the picket fence next door, the shutters on a house down the block, the milk truck making its rounds. They are part of all the sounds and sights that mean home to me.

Sometimes we have to look beneath the surface to find real beauty. Watching sparrows reassures me that this search is well worth the effort.

Potluck

Imagine a dinner with over one hundred dishes!

Appetizers to tempt the eye as well as the palate, succulent meats dripping gravy, desserts that would do honor to any chef's reputation. Is it a sultan's banquet? Dinner at the White House? A restaurant tour of New York? No. None of these. It's a potluck dinner.

I have never been to a potluck that didn't turn out to be a gourmet feast. It's a feast in cellophane and plastic containers — but splendid just the same. Perhaps that's why my knees turn to — well — spaghetti whenever I'm asked to contribute a dish to one of these. Not that I don't cook up a fairly tasty concoction myself. But compared to my neighbor's authentic Greek pastry shaped like the Parthenon, my trusty noodle dish looks pretty ordinary.

I brought "old trusty" to the last potluck I attended. It was an affair for charity, and I hoped everyone would have the charity to eat my cooking. As I stood in line, I admired the spectrum of puddings and casseroles and approached my own with dread. What if no one had touched it? What if it turned out to be the only dish left uneaten? I nervously glanced over at the end of the table.

There it was, but my casserole dish was empty! I might even add that someone had scraped the last bits from the bottom.

I think this goes to show that we have to trust our own abilities. Very often, it takes something small — like a casserole — to point that out!

A Building Grows Up

We all can't be lucky enough to work or live near a construction site. But during the last two years, a large office building went up close to my job. Each evening as I left for home, I would pause and note its progress. At first there was merely a big hole in the ground. Then slowly the structure began to take shape and develop a personality all its own. As if some wizard had waved his magic wand, the concrete and steel fell into place. Floor by floor the building rose until I had to lean over backwards to see the top.

When it was finally finished and open, I took a couple of walks inside and listened to the comments of others inspecting the offices and lobbies. Like a doting parent, I was quite indignant when I overheard negative remarks. I watched that building grow up and felt as if I had played a part in its development.

Some people might think it's silly to treat a building as if it were human. But to me, a building really *is* human, for it's something humanity has been able to create. Concrete and brick are only as cold and impersonal as we want to make them.

Hot Dog!

Is there anyone who doesn't like hot dogs? I don't think so. And the hot dog that tastes best to me is the one I gobble down at a baseball game. Sitting in the stands watching the plays, I find myself growing hungrier and hungrier. Perhaps it's all the shouting and cheering and hand clapping that does it. By the time the third inning begins, I'm famished. And famished for one thing only — a nice, juicy, hot dog.

If I'm lucky, a vendor is nearby. Usually it takes him about ten minutes to come my way. Ten long, hungry minutes.

"Hot dog, hey, hot dog — over here," I yell as I spot his white coat down the aisle. Victory is in sight. After much hand waving, pointing and passing back and forth of money, it's mine — that lovely, rosy hunk of sausage, cuddled in a baby-soft bun, with the crowning touch of creamy golden mustard! Ahh — I've never eaten anything so good.

Some people may turn their noses up at the humble hot dog. But they'll never convince the fans happily munching away that there's anything better. Hot dogs — maybe *they're* really the great American pastime!

Let's Get It Straight

My walls are covered with paintings and prints that are either three inches too high, a bit far to the left, or centered only when you look at them with your head tipped at a thirty-degree angle. In other words, I can't seem to hang a picture straight.

My friends tell me it doesn't matter. Nobody will notice. But I notice. And somehow I feel I have an obligation to the artist to hang his or her creation just right. We are partners — the artist and I. It's my duty to uphold my half of the bargain.

So recently when I purchased a new print, I was determined to hang it perfectly. "Let's see now," I thought. "Allow two inches at the top for the wire. It should be centered here. No, a little more to the left, a little higher. There." Holding my breath, I marked two spots where the nails would go and, before I could change my mind or call for help, hammered them into the wall. Then I slid the wire carefully into place and stood back. It was perfect!

We can't all be artists. But every time I look at that print, I feel good, knowing the artist did his part — and I did mine!

A Bicycle Built For One

My bicycle has decorated the back wall of my garage for the last ten years. Although I must admit it makes an outstanding and novel wall hanging, I decided to put it to better use. In other words, I was going to try and ride it!

Monday was too hot for riding. Tuesday, too cold. Wednesday the wind blew in the wrong direction. But Thursday put an end to procrastination. Sunny, seventy degrees, Thursday was a bike rider's dream. That is, if I could still ride. Ten years is a long time between trips.

As I walked the bike outside to check it over and put air in the tires, I heard a little voice inside my head saying, "Don't worry. Bike riding is something we never forget."

"Ha! Is that so?" I answered the little voice. "It may be something *you* never forget, but as for me, I'm not so sure."

Finding the bike in ridable condition, I tried out the seat. "Not a bad fit," I thought. "So far, so good." Then I gave a little shove off the ground with my left foot, felt for the pedals, teetered a few seconds to the left, to the right, until — there was no doubt about it — I was riding again!

"I told you so," the little voice said with a smug chuckle.

Within us all is a deep well of skills we haven't drawn upon for years. One person might have loved to ice-skate as a child, another to play volleyball, paint, write or recite all the state capitals by heart. Learning to do something for the first time is very satisfying, but isn't it even more fun the second or third time around? When we return to a hobby or sport we once loved...we're really welcoming back an old friend.

A Dash of Music

I usually listen to the news while I cook dinner. But since my radio broke a few weeks ago, I have turned to the stereo and to an old and much neglected friend — Mozart. I had gotten out of the habit of listening to music. It used to be as much a part of my life as cornflakes. But with work and home chores, I found less and less time for it until I was barely using my records at all.

The broken radio gave me the perfect opportunity to begin listening again. As I cut meat and peeled potatoes, the crisp melody of the "Eine Kleine Nachtmusik" filled every corner of the kitchen with its lilting energy. "How could I have given this up?" I asked myself as I worked. "I've been missing so much." I hummed along with violins, tapped my fingers against the counter top. Cooking dinner had never before been such a beautiful experience.

The melody of a violin, the grace of a dancer or the symmetry of a painting lift our spirits above the routine of daily existence. Peeling potatoes? It's a delight...with a little help from Mozart!

One More Square

Mountain climbing frightens me, so I solve crossword puzzles instead. This analogy may be a bit exaggerated, but to crossword addicts — and there are millions — puzzle solving is serious business. An empty square cries out to be filled just as a mountain cries out to be climbed. It's a call that keeps us up all night long combing through the dictionary, encyclopedia, thesaurus — anything — just to find a solution. Filling every last square is a challenge that never gets stale.

Some people say they work these puzzles because they like to learn new words or enjoy the mental exercise. These reasons are true enough, but I think people solve puzzles for the tremendous sense of accomplishment they feel when there are no empty boxes left. Puzzles remind us that even the smallest challenge can make the difference between an ordinary day or one that is special.

Quiet Times

We all need quiet times... corners of the day when we can think about our lives — where we're going, where we've been. A friend tells me her favorite quiet moment comes at about six in the morning, before the house is awake. This precious time gives her the chance to write her husband a silly note, read an article she's been saving or just watch the world outside come alive.

My best quiet times happen when it rains — especially in the springtime. The first drops of moisture invite me to put on a raincoat and take a long walk. As I splash through puddles and watch the silvery streams of water slide down sidewalk cracks, I find myself, like the earth, awakening inside. This is when I evaluate the past year and ponder the world around me, the world inside me. I make plans to expand my goals, hobbies, friendships, loves.

Whatever the season, the rain is my cue to stop what I'm doing — if only for a minute — and reflect on things that are important to me. It's not easy to find uncluttered moments in our days. But they are a gift well worth the effort — a gift only we can give ourselves.

Bargains Galore

I can't resist the lure of a sale. It doesn't matter if I don't need or want the merchandise being offered. The minute I spot a "reduced" sign near a counter or rack, I'm hooked. Because of this, my wardrobe contains a pair of magenta tennis shoes, a feather boa and ten lace handkerchiefs monogrammed with the letter *Q*!

But I do find some good bargains, too. Bargain hunting is a game I play very well. I say "game" because that's how I see it. Step one comes when I spot an item — say a blouse or skirt — that I really want. However, because it is not on sale, buying it at this point is unthinkable. Step two is the initial test of skill. It is the time of waiting — watching the newspaper for ads, and inspecting the rack at least once a week. Step three brings the first sale. The coveted item is reduced at last — but not enough. This is the moment when the question "To buy or not to buy" hangs heavily over my head. Step six separates the amateurs from the professionals. The item is now available for half price. The amateur will get to the store in five minutes flat with money in hand. Not the pro. It takes true grit to wait for the final "two-thirds reduced" sign to appear.

When we figure out how to make the most of an opportunity — even a small one — we can't help feeling like winners! The sense of pride is hard to match and — at two-thirds off — it's not even expensive.

A Cat at the Door

Most cats behave as if they couldn't care less about us. Once in a while, however, if we mortals are good, they may surprise us.

Yesterday, as I ambled up the walk after work, I noticed a furry little face in the window. "Could it be that my cat is actually greeting me?" I asked myself, and then quickly dismissed the thought. Sasha had never done that before. Why spoil me now? She had trained me, as all cats train their owners, not to expect anything. I put the key in the lock, opened the door and tripped over a lump in front of me. Sasha! There she was, standing right in the foyer. And as an added bit of cream on the pudding, so to speak, she honored me with an affectionate "Mew." This was too much to be believed.

"A mirage?" I wondered. But no. A mirage can't rub its head against your leg. A mirage can't be petted.

Sasha got her favorite dinner last night. Because she gave me her version of the "red carpet"? Well, yes. But more for pointing out that love often comes when we least expect it.

New Things Everywhere

We all love new things. They don't have to be big or expensive like a car or a mink coat; just little, ordinary things we use every day.

When I was a child, new crayons thrilled me more than anything else. The pictures I colored always seemed to look brighter if I used perfectly pointed crayons that came from a box with the lid still intact.

Now, in my adult world, I don't use crayons much. But I get that same tingly feeling from other new things, such as pencils sharpened for the first time, a box of stationery that still has all the matching envelopes in it, and freshly painted lines on the street. Yes — that's right. When the lines are all shiny and slick, unsmudged by wheels and the weather, it's as if the street has been given a face-lift. Gives me a lift, too!

We can't always afford to go out and buy something new for ourselves. But if we look, we'll find "new" things to enjoy all around us — a thick towel still warm from the dryer, the grand opening of a supermarket or the first rainbow of spring wild flowers. "New" doesn't have to cost us a cent.

Love Ya

He's always leaving little notes around. Just the other day, I opened my purse and found one tucked inside.

"I wanted you to know," it read, "that next to my Porsche, I love you best." Signed "Beethoven."

I chuckled as I put this note in the box with the others he's written. I'd teased him about his car the night before. This message was his way of gently teasing me back — with love. A note — it's a small thing, but to me it's an act of love.

The little daily efforts to please, the actions that show we care — they build a foundation of love that can last a lifetime.

Adding A Rose

The "decorating demon" inside of me comes to life once a year. When this happens, every room in my house seems painted with the same color — drab — and filled with the same style furniture — outdated! The whole place screams out for new carpets, new drapes, new chairs and new tables. Unfortunately, my budget does some screaming of its own, especially when it's stretched to its limit. And this year, the decorating urge struck me just when my budget wasn't stretching very far. But still, these urges don't die easily, so I decided to succumb to temptation and decorate my heart out — as long as I didn't spend more than fifteen dollars!

What could I do for fifteen dollars? I could buy wallpaper for one wall but, on the other hand, I'm a terrible paperhanger. I could reupholster one cushion of the sofa, but what about the other two? I could carpet two square feet of the spare bedroom, but that would leave a lot of space looking pretty bare. I couldn't figure out what to fix or paint or replace until I spotted the perfect solution in a small curio shop near my home.

It was a delicate china rose with pale yellow

petals, finely veined leaves on a gracefully curving stem and even tiny thorns. About eight inches long, the rose was designed to rest on its side like a goddess on a chaise longue. I loved it at first sight. I don't have many knickknacks in my living room, so there were at least three tabletops to choose from that would look beautiful wearing a rose.

It seems that we don't really have to turn our whole world topsy-turvy to satisfy a desire for a change in our surroundings. Rearranging the photos on the dresser, taking an alternate route to work, switching hairstyles — all of these add a touch of variety to life. These are little things, of course. But they add up to a whole lot of good feelings...inside.

Set in Plantin, a typeface designed by F. H. Pierpont.
Printed on Hallmark Eggshell Book paper.
Book design and titles by Rick Cusick.